WHAT DO YOU THINK?

A Kid's Guide to Dealing with Daily Dilemmas

WRITTEN BY LINDA SCHWARTZ
ILLUSTRATED BY BEVERLY ARMSTRONG
EDITED BY SHERRI M. BUTTERFIELD

The Learning Works

Creative Teaching Press, Inc.
Huntington Beach, CA 92649

Library of Congress Catalog Number: 92-074103
ISBN 0-88160-224-8
LW 221

Printed in the United States of America

Dedication

This book is dedicated to
Steve, Mike, Nathaniel, and Tobey
and to kids everywhere
to help them learn
how to get along with others and
to help them discover
more about themselves.

Acknowledgments

My sincere thanks to Carl and Lois Conn of Knowledge Industries for the suggestions that motivated me to write this book and for their support over the years. Special thanks to the following people for their valuable comments and contributions: Phyllis Amerikaner, Rae Aronoff, Kimberley Clark, Alicia Dondero, Ph.D., Angela Antenore Sponder, and Bobbie Vidal. Thanks to Sherri Butterfield for her editorial expertise, and to Beverly Armstrong for the delightful illustrations that enliven the pages of this book.

Contents

A Note to Kids 11–12
A Note to Parents and Teachers...13–14

AT HOME 15–54
Respecting Privacy......................17–18
Using Your Allowance 19–20
Choosing a Hairstyle...................21–22
Sick Pet 23–24
Fighting in the Car 25–26
Visiting Grandma 27–28
A Rule Against TV........................29–30
Dad's New Friend.........................31–32
Missing a Deadline 33–34
Respecting Property.....................35–36

Homework Habits.......................37–38
Schedule Conflict 39–40
Sharing Space 41–42
Sparing Feelings........................43–44
Prejudiced Remarks 45–46
Talking on the Phone...................47–48
Loud Music 49–50
Abusing a Drug 51–52
Drinking Alcohol.........................53–54

AT SCHOOL AND ON THE WAY 55–110
Setting Priorities........................57–58
Smoking......................................59–60

Contents
(continued)

Competing for a Part 61–62
Name Calling...........................63–64
Biased Teacher........................65–66
Group Report 67–68
Holiday Pageant.......................69–70
Gossip 71–72
Vandals 73–74
Difficult Name 75–76
Bullies 77–78
Racial Discrimination................79–80
Forging a Note 81–82
Getting Involved 83–84

Coping with Diabetes 85–86
Being Ignored 87–88
Native Dress 89–90
Copying a Report 91–92
Biased Views 93–94
Handling Humiliation 95–96
Ethnic Food 97–98
Stolen Bicycle..........................99–100
Choosing a Team 101–102
Cheating on a Test.................103–104
Living with HIV 105–106
Language Barrier 107–108

Contents
(continued)

Incorrect Grade........................109–110

OUT ON YOUR OWN........**111–144**
Forbidden Friend 113–114
Soccer versus Services............115–116
Following the Crowd 117–118
Unwelcome Touching..............119–120
Smoking Marijuana 121–122
Movie Restrictions 123–124
Property Damage.....................125–126
On Your Honor 127–128
Defending a Friend 129–130

Lying About Your Age 131–132
Shoplifting 133–134
Being a Vegetarian 135–136
Pocketing the Money 137–138
Trying New Foods 139–140
Ethnic Jokes 141–142
Pirating a Disk 143–144

IN YOUR COMMUNITY...**145–170**
Too Many Animals 147–148
Using Polystyrene 149–150
Helping the Needy 151–152

Contents
(continued)

Toxic Waste...........................153–154
Cutting Down Trees...............155–156
Anti-Semitism.......................157–158
Animal Research....................159–160
Destroying Nature..................161–162
Staging a Protest....................163–164
A Better Neighborhood............165–166
Six-Pack Rings......................167–168
In a Wheelchair.....................169–170

WITHIN YOURSELF..........**171–179**
Resolving Conflicts 173
Who Are You?................................174
How Do You Rate As a Friend? 175
Tips on Making Friends..........176–177
Hints on How to Be a Friend 178
A Friendly Gesture 179
Index **180–184**

A Note to Kids

Life is full of dilemmas—situations in which you must choose between alternatives and make decisions. Sometimes these decisions seem simple to make, like how to wear your hair, how to spend your money, or how loud to play your music. But even seemingly simple decisions can cause problems. Suppose, for example, that your dad does not like the hairstyle you choose, that you do not have enough money for all of the things you want to buy, or that the sounds which are music to your ears are noise to your neighbors'.

Situations of this kind result in conflict. **Conflict** is the tension or struggle caused by opposing ideas, needs, wants, or demands. Being in the midst of conflict can be very uncomfortable. You may feel as if you are being pushed one way and pulled another. This awkward, undecided, and often painful position is described as being "on the horns of a dilemma."

Conflict can occur between enemies or friends, among family members, and even within yourself. Because conflict is common, you need to know how to deal with it successfully. To resolve conflict, you can make a choice between opposing ideas, seek a compromise that allows you to combine the best of both, or come up with a whole new idea.

This book asks **What Do You Think?** about ordinary things like sharing space, sparing feelings, talking on the phone, and respecting privacy and about more difficult issues like abusing drugs, cheating on a test, and following the crowd. The author

A Note to Kids
(continued)

describes dilemmas you might face at home, at school and on the way, out on your own, or within yourself.

First, select and read one of these dilemmas. Next—before you turn the page—give the dilemma some thought. Ask yourself how *you* would resolve this conflict. Then, turn the page. Read the statements and consider the questions that are listed. Ask yourself if these statements and questions are the same as those you thought of. Did you have some additional ideas? Finally, talk over these ideas—both the ones listed in the book and the ones you thought of—with

other members of your family.

Your life is a chain of choices and the consequences that follow naturally from those choices. One way to control your own life is by making your own choices. The way to make your life better is by making better choices. If you resolve a conflict by making a choice you later regret, you can learn from this experience and make a wiser choice next time.

The purpose of this book is to help you think about choice-making situations—dilemmas—in advance so that you will be better prepared to deal wisely with them if and when they arise.

A Note to Parents and Teachers

In the course of growing up, most children encounter a variety of dilemmas—situations in which they must make decisions—when they are at home, when they are at school, and when they are out on their own. If children are alone in these situations, they must make decisions and resolve the associated conflicts with little or no on-the-spot guidance from the parents, teachers, or other adults who care about them.

The purpose of **What Do You Think?** is to prepare children to make decisions and resolve conflicts *before* the need arises. It provides children with a list of questions and statements they can consider to help them understand their feelings, clarify their values, and develop skill in evaluating options, considering consequences, and making choices.

Of course, no book can be all things to all children because no one author can imagine all possible dilemmas, anticipate all probable approaches, and/or describe all practicable options. For these reasons, **What Do You Think?** presents ideas to consider in making choices but does not tell the reader how to think or what to choose.

While **What Do You Think?** is *not* moralistic, some issues may pose moral dilemmas. The basic premises of this book are (1) that you are responsible for your own life, (2) that the way to be in control of your life is to make your own choices, (3) that the way to have a better life is to make wiser choices, and (4) that you can learn to make wiser choices in the future by examining your unwise choices of the past and preparing in advance for the choices yet to come.

Encourage the children in your care to read one of these situation descriptions and—before turning the page—to think about what choices they would make and what actions they would take if they found themselves on the horns of this particular dilemma. Select the dilemmas to be examined and modify your consideration of the related questions and statements to make them relevant to your particular family or classroom situation and appropriate for the maturity levels and abilities of your children.

Once the children have decided what they would do, tell them to turn the page and check their ideas against the ones that are listed. Help the children compare their ideas

A Note to Parents and Teachers
(continued)

with those in the book. Talk about specific similarities and differences and the reasons for them. Help them to consider carefully the advantages and disadvantages of each option and make them aware of the possible consequences of their choices.

The dilemmas described in this book make ideal topics for discussion. Situation descriptions can be used to spark dinner table conversation, to pass idle hours while traveling, to replace television programs and video games as a source of entertainment, or to fill the final restless moments before the school bell rings.

Several situation descriptions can be combined to create special study units. For example, the situations on pages 69–70, 75–76, 79–80, 89–90, 93–94, 97–98, 107–108, and 141–142 might be used as part of a unit designed to help children understand differences and appreciate diversity. In conjunction with this unit, children might be encouraged to find out which country their own ancestors came from and to talk about food, clothing, and customs as reflections of culture. Similarly, the situations on other pages might be combined to create units on such topics as The Dangers of Strangers, On Your Honor, Substance Abuse, Your Habits and Your Health, and Ready, Set, Study!

In group settings, these situations can be used for role playing and for cooperative learning. For example, parts can be assigned and children can be encouraged to pantomime a particular dilemma or to turn this dilemma into a one-act play by creating original dialogue.

In addition to descriptions of more than seventy situations, this book contains a five-page index and tips on how to get to know yourself, how to resolve conflicts, how to make friends, and how to be a friend.

Children who learn to view life's dilemmas as opportunities for making choices are more likely to choose wisely, suffer fewer negative consequences, establish more meaningful relationships, and create better lives for themselves and those around them.

At Home

In this section you will find descriptions of situations that may cause conflicts in your home, among family members, or between neighbors. These situations include

talking on the phone,

using your allowance,

choosing a hairstyle,

respecting privacy,

sharing space,

and missing a deadline.

First, select and read one of these situations. You can go in any order. Next, think about what you would do. Then, turn the page. Read and consider the statements and questions that are listed. Finally, talk over these ideas with your family. Discuss how you would feel and what you might do in a similar situation.

Respecting Privacy

Each time you are away,
your younger sister
comes into your bedroom and
goes through your belongings,
even though you have asked her
repeatedly to stay out.

Respecting Privacy

✱ How does it make you feel when your sister ignores your request to stay out of your room?

✱ Why do you think she wants to come into your room?

✱ Would it help to talk with your sister about how she would feel if *you* went through *her* things while she was away?

✱ Are there things you could do to encourage her to stay out of your room?

✱ Would it help if you made a "Please Do Not Disturb" sign for your bedroom door?

✱ When might you involve someone else in helping you with this situation? To whom would you talk? What would you say?

Using Your Allowance

You have been saving
your allowance
for several months.
Just when you have
enough money
for the computer game
you really want,
your brother asks you
to chip in on a gift
for your mom.

Using Your Allowance

* What options do you have to resolve this situation?

* Would you discuss your dilemma with your brother? What would you say to him?

* How would you feel about waiting to buy the computer game or buying a less expensive gift for your mother?

* Are there gifts you could give your mom that don't cost money?

Choosing a Hairstyle

You want to get your hair
cut in the latest style
like all of your friends.
Your dad forbids you
to do so.

Choosing a Hairstyle

* Why do you want to wear your hair this way?

* Should grown-ups tell kids how to wear their hair? Why would parents care how their children wear their hair?

* A style that is flattering on one person may look awful on another. Is this particular hairstyle a good choice? Have you considered how it will look on *you*?

* Have you thought about how long it will take for your hair to return to its original color or grow back to its previous length?

* Is there a compromise between what you want and what your dad wants?

Sick Pet

Your dog has been with your family
since before you were born.
A veterinarian discovers that
your pet has a fatal disease.
Your parents want to have the dog
put to sleep to end his suffering.

Sick Pet

* Losing a pet is painful. Talk about your feelings with your mom or dad, or with a friend who has lost a dog or cat and will understand.

* Think about the good times you had with your dog. Recalling the happy moments the two of you spent together may help you feel less sad.

* Do you think getting a new puppy would help? Nothing can replace the relationship you had with your old dog, but would having another animal to care for help you get over your loss?

* Find ways to express the feelings you have about your pet, such as writing a story or poem about your dog or making a scrapbook. What else can you do to show how you feel about your pet?

RANGER
246 E. OAK ST.
DEERVILLE
213 2140

Fighting in the Car

You and the other kids in your family always fight
during long car trips.
This time your mom or dad has asked *you*
to help keep the peace.

Fighting in the Car

✱ How do you feel about being in charge of this situation?

✱ Why do you think your brothers and sisters fight in the car? What might help them get along better?

✱ Can you think of some games and activities that can be played in the car to keep passengers of all ages amused?

✱ What ground rules would you establish for your brothers and sisters? How would you get them to agree to the rules you suggest?

✱ When you stop, try switching seats so that family members take turns riding up front or sitting beside the windows.

Visiting Grandma

Your mom wants you
to accompany her
each week when she
visits your grandmother
in a nursing home.
You love your grandmother
but would rather
go to the mall
with your friends.

Visiting Grandma

* Would you tell your mother how you feel? What would you say to her?

* What are your options in this situation?

* How do you feel about seeing your grandmother in the nursing home?

* Are there things you can do for your grandmother between visits to let her know that you are thinking of her and that you care about her?

April 12

Dear Grandma,

Remember when you showed me how to make strawberry jam the summer I stayed with you? That was fun. And yesterday I made jam by myself for the first time ever! It's not as good as yours, but even Josh said he likes it —and he's picky!

I'll bring you some jam and biscuits when I come see you Tuesday.

Love,
☺ Annie

A Rule Against TV

Your dad wants to make a new rule
against watching television on school nights.

A Rule Against TV

* Why do you think your father wants to make this rule? Could you talk to your dad about it?

* How much time do you spend watching television? How much time do you spend reading, practicing, studying, or taking part in sports? Keep track of your activities for a week. You may be surprised at the results.

* Is there room for a compromise? See if your dad will allow you to watch television on alternate nights or to watch one show each evening *after* you have finished your homework.

SATURDAY MAY 22	
ACTIVITY	TOTAL
EXERCISE	
SOCCER 1-3 P.M.	2½
BIKE RIDE 6:30-7 P.M.	
CHORES	
9-11:30 A.M.	2½
TROMBONE PRACTICE	
11:30-12 A.M.	½
READING	0
TV 7:30-9 A.M. (1½)	6
4-5:30 P.M. (1½)	
7-10 P.M. (3)	

Dad's New Friend

Your parents have recently divorced. You have a
starring role in the school play and have invited
both of your parents to be in the audience
on opening night. Your dad wants to bring his new
girl friend. You know her presence will make your mom
feel angry and hurt.

Dad's New Friend

* How do you feel about having both of your parents at the play?

* How can your parents work this out so no one is uncomfortable on opening night?

* Is the play being performed more than once? How important is it to you to have them both at the play opening night?

Missing a Deadline

You have not finished
a social studies report
that is due tomorrow.
You are thinking about
pretending to be sick
so that you can stay home
to complete the assignment.

Missing a Deadline

* Can you think of other ways to handle this situation so that you will not have to pretend to be sick when you are really well? For example, what would happen if you told your teacher the truth and asked to be given an extension?

* What would be gained by pretending to be sick? What are some of the costs?

* What can you do differently in the future so that you will meet the next deadline?

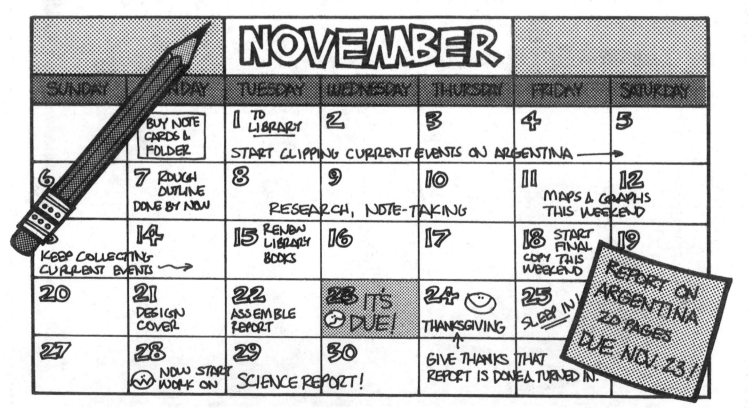

Respecting Property

Your older brother has asked you not to use his favorite video game. A friend of yours is spending the night at your house and wants to play that game. The friend says that your brother is gone and won't know the difference.

Respecting Property

✱ If you let your friend play with your brother's video game, what might the consequences be?

✱ What are other options you and your friend have?

✱ How could you discuss this with your brother? What kind of compromise could you make the next time this situation comes up?

✱ How would you feel if someone in your family used something of yours without your permission?

Homework Habits

You are more comfortable
doing your homework assignments while sprawled
on your bedroom floor,
listening to loud music.
Your folks want you to study at your desk
with the music turned off.

Homework Habits

✳ Why do you think your parents want you to study the way they suggest?

✳ Are your study habits affecting the quality of your schoolwork? Can you write neatly while lying on the floor? Can you concentrate while listening to music? Why do you like to study your way?

✳ How could you and your parents resolve the issue of how you study?

Schedule Conflict

You have been looking forward
to participating with your mom
in a mother-daughter softball game.
Just before the big event,
she tells you that
a meeting she can't miss
has been scheduled
for the same day and time.

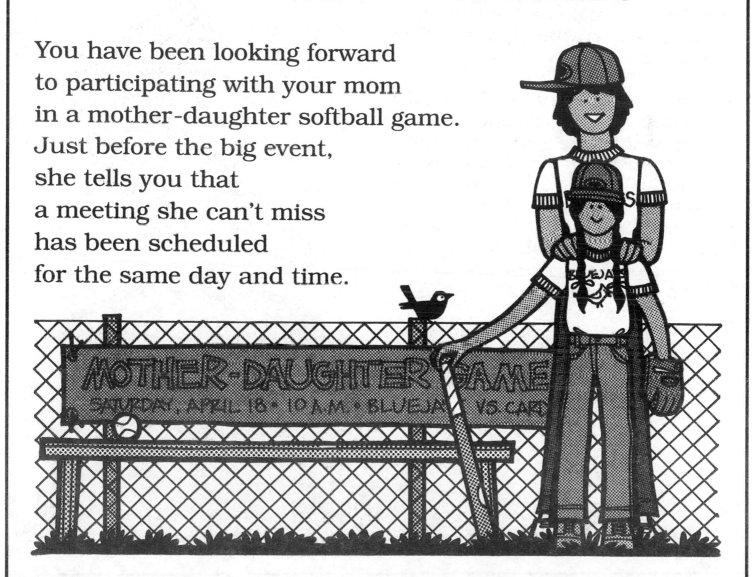

Schedule Conflict

✱ How does the sudden change in plans make you feel? How do you think it makes your mom feel?

✱ Because no one can be in two places at once, it is frequently necessary to make choices between activities that are scheduled at the same time. In this instance, which activity should take priority, work or play? Why? What might be the consequences if your mom chose to play in the game instead of going to the meeting?

✱ Would the way your mother tells you she can't come to your game make a difference in how you feel?

✱ Is there anyone else you could ask to take your mom's place in the game such as a relative or a close friend?

Sharing Space

Your brother is reading a book
in his favorite chair in the family room.
You want to use that room to watch
the only television set in the house.
You ask your brother to leave,
but he refuses and says that
he was there first.

Sharing Space

* Why do you think your brother should leave the room?

* Is there another place your brother could go to read? How would you suggest to your brother that he go there?

* Does your family have a schedule for TV viewing? If not, could you work one out for your family?

Sparing Feelings

Last year your grandmother
knit a sweater for you
for your birthday.
You don't like this garment
and have never worn it.
Now your grandmother
is staying with you for a week
while your parents are out of town.
You know that she expects to see
you wear the sweater.

Sparing Feelings

* What will you say if your grandmother asks you how you like the sweater?

* Would you be willing to wear the sweater once or twice during your grandmother's visit—even though you do not like it—so that her feelings will not be hurt?

* If your grandmother does not see you in the sweater, she may ask why you are *not* wearing it. What will you say?

Prejudiced Remarks

You pass by your sister's room
while she is talking on the phone.
You overhear her make unkind remarks
about members of a particular
minority ethnic group.

Prejudiced Remarks

✱ Why do you think your sister made those comments?

✱ Why is it a problem when remarks of this kind are made?

✱ Should you talk to your sister about this incident or should you ignore it? If you decide to talk to her, what would you say? How do you think she would respond?

✱ Should you involve your parents in the matter or keep it just between you two?

✱ To be **prejudiced** against a group means judging the members of this group and forming negative opinions about them *before* getting to know them. Sometimes people make prejudiced remarks about a particular group because they are ignorant of the group's customs or jealous of its achievements. Perhaps, if your sister had a greater understanding of the history and culture of this particular ethnic group, she would be less likely to make remarks of this kind in the future.

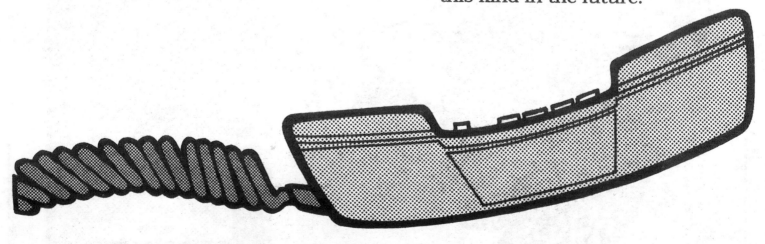

Talking on the Phone

Your teenage sister
likes to talk
on the telephone.
When she is home,
the phone is always busy.
No one can get through
to anyone else
in your family.

Talking on the Phone

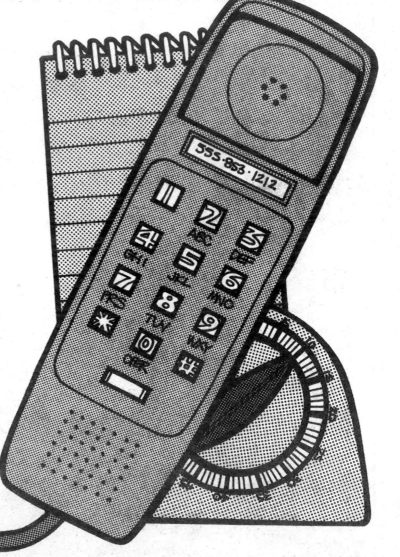

* What suggestions could you make to help deal with this situation? Are these suggestions fair to both you and your sister?

* What do you think your parents would propose? Would their ideas be different from or similar to yours?

* Can you think of situations that could pose problems for your family if someone couldn't get through to your home because the phone was constantly in use?

Loud Music

A teenager who lives next door
plays an electric guitar
at all hours of the night.
His loud music keeps you awake.
It also disturbs your family
and your neighbors.

Loud Music

* The teenager is playing the guitar inside his own home. Does this fact give him the right to play the music whenever he likes? What do you think? What does the law say?

* What is the best way to gain the cooperation of this teenager? Should you talk to him since you are about his age?

* Are there some compromises that can be made concerning when and how loud the music is played so that the teenager can play his guitar *and* you can get your sleep?

* If your efforts to gain cooperation fail, what might you do and whom could you call?

* Should your parents talk to this teenager? Would he be more inclined to listen to adults?

* Should all of the neighbors who have been bothered by this teenager's loud music join together to solve the problem? What might be the advantages and disadvantages of this approach?

Abusing a Drug

Your parents frequently use an illegal drug.
This drug has changed the way they act
and has made your home life miserable.
You love your parents and wonder
how to get help for them.

Abusing a Drug

✱ How do you feel about your parents using drugs?

✱ Why do adults and teenagers use drugs? What could they do instead?

✱ Consider the advantages and disadvantages of taking action. What your parents are doing is harmful to them and to you. Is there something you can do that will change this situation for the better? In the long run, how will your parents feel about your taking action?

✱ Are there adults in your life you could turn to for help or advice?

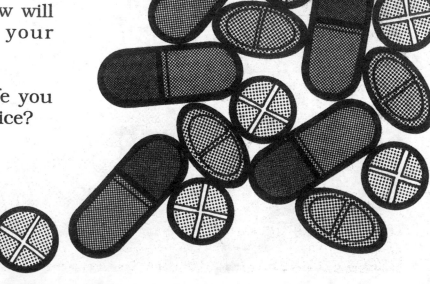

Drinking Alcohol

You discover that your 16-year-old sister has been raiding the liquor cabinet when she comes home at lunchtime with her friends.

Drinking Alcohol

* How do you feel about what your sister is doing?

* Why do you think your sister is drinking alcoholic beverages? What could she do instead?

* Would you let your sister know that you are aware of what she is doing and talk with her about it? Is there someone you could talk to about helping your sister?

* Would you tell your parents about what your sister is doing? Why or why not?

* Is it a parent's responsibility to keep alcoholic beverages away from kids? Why or why not?

At School and On the Way

In this section you will find descriptions of situations that may cause conflicts among friends and classmates at school and on the way. These situations include

being teased,

working on a group report,

forging a note,

setting priorities,

being ignored,

and choosing a team.

First, select and read one of these situations. You can go in any order. Next, think about what you would do. Then, turn the page. Read and consider the statements and questions that are listed. Finally, talk over these ideas with your family. Discuss how you would feel and what you might do in a similar situation.

Setting Priorities

Your coach and teammates are counting on you
to show up for an important practice
before a championship game.
You receive an invitation
to a very special party
that is on the same day
and at the same time
as the practice.

Setting Priorities

* How would your teammates feel if you went to the party? What would you tell your coach?

* Could you divide your time between the practice and the party so that you are able to go to both?

* If another member of the team chose to go to the party while you went to the practice, how would you feel about your choice? How would you feel about your teammate's choice?

* How do you set priorities? When events conflict, how do you decide which one is more important? How do you choose between them?

Smoking

During afternoon recess,
you go into the school restroom
and find two friends smoking cigarettes.

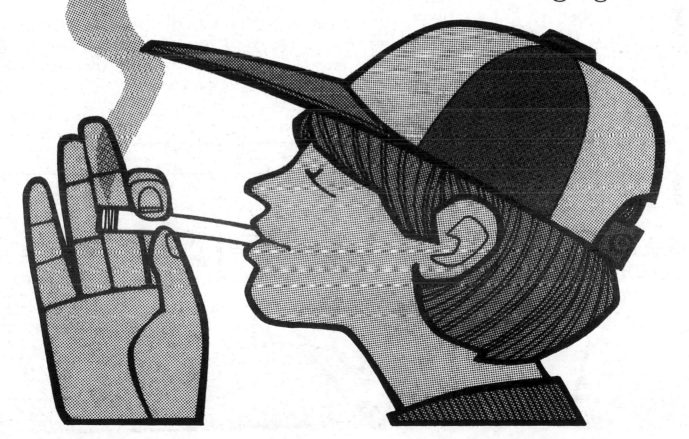

Smoking

* How do you feel about what your friends are doing?

* Is it any of your business? Why or why not?

* If you choose to get involved, do you think the matter should be just between you and your two friends, or should an adult be told?

* If you tell an adult, how do you think your friends would react? What would you say to them?

* Does your school have a rule against smoking in restrooms? If so, what are the consequences for someone who breaks the rule?

* Do you know what damage smoking causes to the human body? How could you find out more about the effects of smoking on your health?

* Do you think your friends are aware of the risks associated with smoking? If so, why do you think they choose to do it?

Competing for a Part

You have been looking forward
to trying out for the lead role
in the annual school play.
You discover that your best friend
plans to audition for the same part.

Competing for a Part

* Would this situation be a problem for you? Why or why not?

* Should either you or your friend give up trying out for the part?

* In what ways might your friendship be affected if both you and your friend try out for the same part and only one of you gets it?

* Are there other parts in the play that one or both of you might enjoy?

Name Calling

Kids at school tease you
and call you names
because you have large ears
that stick out.

Name Calling

* How do you react when the kids call you names? What could you do about their teasing?

* Do you care what others think about the way you look? Why or why not?

* Have you ever asked the kids who call you names *why* they do it? It would take some courage to ask, but the question might surprise *them* and their answers might enlighten *you.*

* Have you ever called someone a name? Why did you do it? How did it make you feel? How do you think the other person felt?

Biased Teacher

In science class, the teacher makes sarcastic remarks about girls and doesn't call on them as often as he does the boys.

Biased Teacher

* Do you think the teacher is aware of his behavior? Why or why not?

* Why do you think he makes sarcastic remarks?

* How do his remarks make you feel? How does it feel to not be called on when you want to participate in class discussions?

* Who would you talk to about this situation—your science teacher, your mom or dad, the principal, and/or another teacher?

Group Report

You are working with four classmates
on a group report about Asia.
You know that your teacher plans
to give all members of the group
the same grade.
You also know that
one member of the group
is not doing nearly as much
as the others.

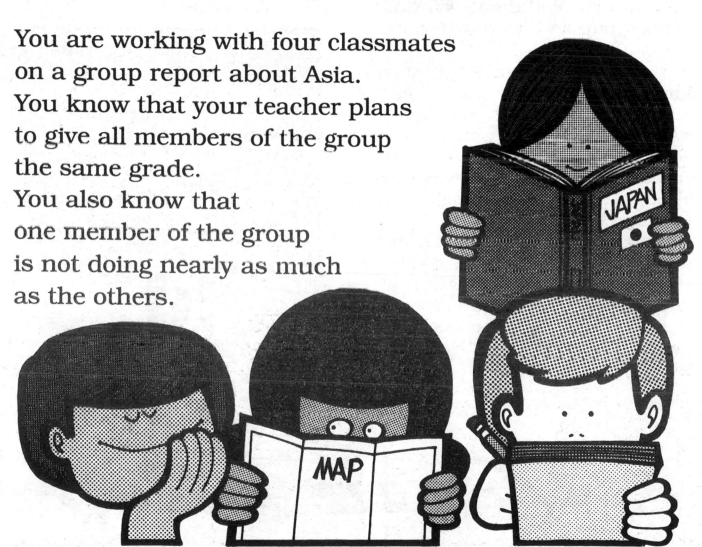

Group Report

* How do you feel about working with a group and sharing a single grade?

* Why do you think the teacher has said you will all get the same grade for this report?

* Has anyone found out why the group member is not doing his or her share? Is there any way you can persuade this student to do more?

* Would you change the way you have divided the topic assignments for the report? Why or why not?

* Would you and the three other members of your group do all of the work so that your grade will not be jeopardized?

* If you and the three other group members do all of the work, should you tell the teacher that the fifth member of your group did not do his or her share? Why or why not?

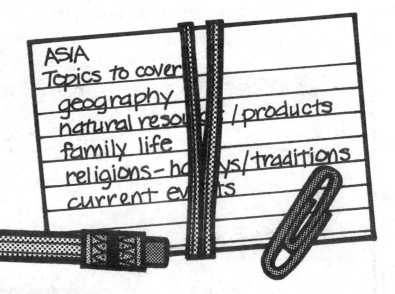

ASIA
Topics to cover
geography
natural resources/products
family life
religions—holidays/traditions
current events

Holiday Pageant

Because of your beliefs,
you do not celebrate Christmas.
Your teacher has asked you to take part
in the class Christmas pageant.

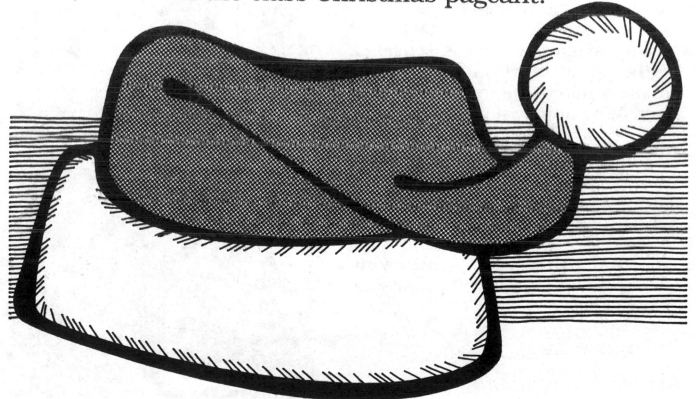

Holiday Pageant

✱ What do you think the conflict is in this situation?

✱ How do you feel about helping to portray a religious story that conflicts with your beliefs?

✱ If the pageant content is *seasonal* rather than *religious*, would that make a difference in the way you feel? Why or why not?

✱ If the pageant is religious and you do *not* feel you can take part in it, how would you feel about becoming involved in other ways?

✱ In what other ways could you participate without compromising your beliefs?

Gossip

You discover that something you told a friend in strict confidence was the topic of conversation during lunch at school.

Gossip

* What bothers you most about this incident, the fact that many people now know your secret or that a friend betrayed your trust?

* Is your friend the *only* person who knew your secret? Are you certain that he or she is the one who shared this information?

* How could you discuss this betrayal with your friend? What would you say to help him or her understand how strongly you feel about it?

* Could you trust this friend again? Under what circumstances?

* Have you ever told someone a secret that you promised not to tell? If so, why did you do it?

Vandals

You are serving as one member
of a school committee
that must decide
how to punish
two of your friends
who have been caught
vandalizing your school.

Vandals

✱ Who suffers when schools are vandalized?

✱ What would you consider to be fair consequences for the vandals' actions? Who should pay for the repairs and clean-up? What other ways are there for making up for this loss?

✱ How can you and other members of the committee determine the actual cost of the vandalism?

✱ Would the fact that the vandals are your friends make it difficult for you to vote to take action against them? If so, what would you do as a member of the committee?

Difficult Name

You were born in another country
and you have a first and last name
that are very difficult
to pronounce.
No one at school
ever says them right.

Zdunczyk?
Znudczyk?
Zdunzyck?
Zundzyck?
Zudnzcyk?

Difficult Name

* How do you think this would make you feel?

* Under what circumstances should you ignore the mispronunciations? Under what circumstances should you make an effort to correct them?

* Is there a way you can help others learn and remember how to pronounce your name correctly?

* Do you know the history of your name? Why is your name important to you?

Zebras don't usually nibble candied zucchini, you know!

Bullies

On the way to school,
you see two older boys
grab the lunch
from a younger boy,
who is walking alone.

Bullies

* Should you go to the younger boy's aid?

* Should you encourage the younger boy to report the incident when he gets to school?

* What choices does the younger boy have to avoid problems of this kind in the future?

* Should the boy tell his parents about the incident? How could his parents help?

* Why do older kids pick on younger ones? How does acting this way make the older kids feel? What effect does it have on the younger ones?

Racial Discrimination

Your parents have taught you to respect people of all backgrounds. Some kids at school are giving a boy in your class a hard time because his skin color is different.

Racial Discrimination

* How do you feel about what the kids are doing? How do you think the boy feels?

* Should you ignore the situation or get involved? If you get involved, what would you say to the kids?

* Should your teacher or principal be made aware of this situation?

* Have you ever been in a situation where you felt discriminated against?

Forging a Note

Students who have been absent from school
cannot be admitted to class without a note
signed by their parents. A friend asks you to forge
a note explaining her absence from school
the previous day.

Forging a Note

* Why didn't your friend bring the required note from home? Do you know the real reason for your friend's absence from school?

* Does the reason she was absent make a difference in whether or not you would forge the note?

* What is wrong with forging a note?

* Has your friend considered the consequences to *both* of you if you forge the note and are caught?

* What might happen to your friendship if you refuse to forge the note?

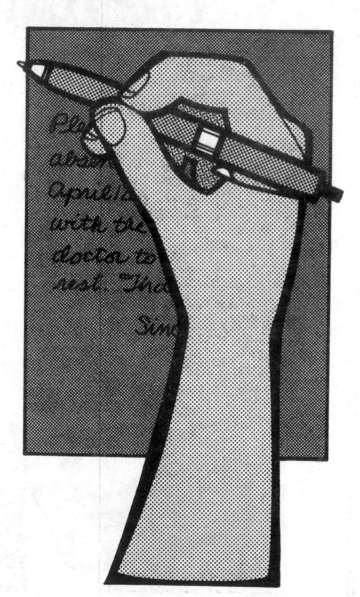

Getting Involved

You overslept and are running late.
While hurrying to school,
you see a young child
take a bad fall
on a bike.

Getting Involved

* Should you risk being late to school so that you can help someone in trouble?

* Will your teacher be understanding about your being tardy?

* If you stop, in what ways can you assist the young child? What real help can you offer?

Coping with Diabetes

Your friend has diabetes and is not supposed to eat sugary foods.

The kids in your class are planning the menu for a Valentine's party. They want to serve cupcakes, punch, and candy.

Coping with Diabetes

* Do you think your friend would want the kids to change or add to the party menu? Why or why not?

* What other things should the people planning the party menu consider?

* What could you or your friend do to help the kids in your class understand diabetes?

* Diabetes is one physical condition that makes it necessary to be careful about what you eat. What other conditions require special attention or diets?

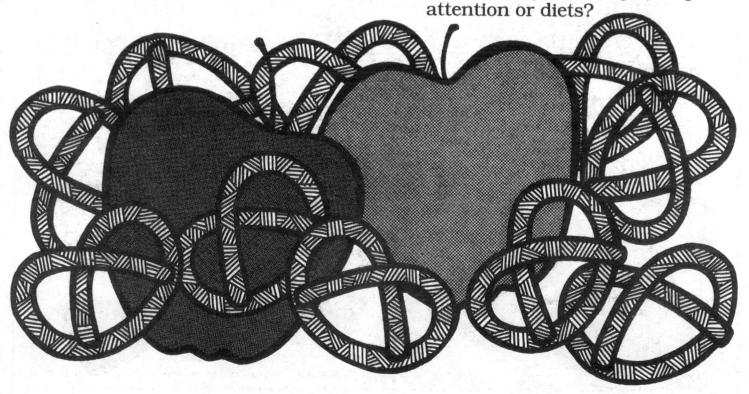

Being Ignored

Your best friend joins the school chorus and ignores you, choosing to spend time and to do things only with other members of this singing group.

Being Ignored

* How would you feel about being ignored by your friend?

* Would you say anything to your friend? If so, what would you say? If no, why not?

* What qualities do you want a friend to have? What things do you expect a friend to do?

* Have you ever intentionally ignored a friend, or made him or her feel left out? Why did you do it?

Native Dress

Your mother, who was born in India,
wears a sari to your school open house.
You overhear several kids in your class
making unkind comments about
the way she dresses.

Native Dress

* Why do some people make fun of the ways in which other people dress?

* Would it be wise to let your classmates know that you are upset by their unkind comments about your mother? What purpose would doing so serve?

* Should you tell your teacher about the incident? What could he or she do? Should you talk to your mother about what happened?

* In what ways might you and your mother help your classmates learn more about the clothing, foods, and customs of her native country?

Copying a Report

Your brother's friend asks
if he can borrow and copy
a social studies report
you wrote last year.
You worked extremely hard
and got a good grade
on that report.

Copying a Report

* How do you feel about sharing the report with your brother's friend?

* Is borrowing someone else's report and turning it in as your own a form of cheating? Why or why not?

* What does your brother's friend learn by borrowing your report instead of doing research and writing his own?

* If you say no to this request, will your brother and his friend be angry? Should you let the reaction you expect from them determine what you choose to do?

* Would *you* ask to copy work that someone else had done?

Biased Views

You and your family come
from a different country.
Your teacher is reading
a book to your class
which portrays
your native country
and its people
in a very negative way.

Biased Views

✳ How does it make you feel to hear this book being read in class? What options do you have in this situation?

✳ Would you talk to your teacher about how you feel? If so, what would you say? When would you choose to talk to him or her?

✳ What could you do to help your classmates view your native country and its people in a more accurate way?

Handling Humiliation

During class, your teacher makes insensitive remarks about you and humiliates you in front of your classmates.

Handling Humiliation

* Why would your teacher do such a thing? What reasons does he or she have for acting in this way?

* How can you let your teacher know how these remarks make you feel?

* If you decide to talk with your teacher, would it be best to do it right away or to wait until after class when there is no one else around? What would you say?

* Would you be wise to tell your parents or the principal about this incident? Why or why not?

Ethnic Food

You and other members
of your family were
born in another country.
Your mom always packs some food
from your native country
in your lunch.
Kids at school tease you and
make fun of what you eat
because it is different.

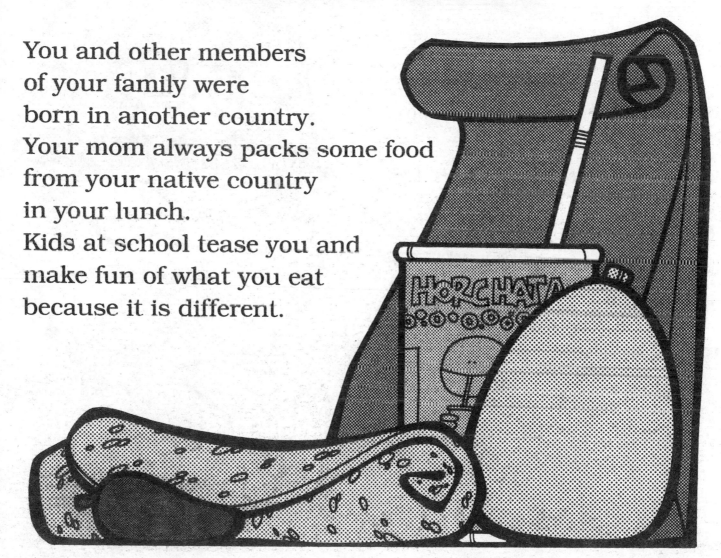

Ethnic Food

* Why do you think the kids tease you about the food you are eating?

* Would you let the kids know they are hurting your feelings? Why or why not?

* What options do you have? Is there anyone you could talk to about the problem?

* What are some examples of foods that you and your family eat that are different from the foods your friends eat?

Stolen Bicycle

Your dad asks you to go to the store to buy a few things
he needs for dinner. Your friend lends you his bicycle
because yours has a flat tire. While you are inside
the grocery store, someone steals the bike.
Your friend uses the bike to get to school each day.

Stolen Bicycle

✱ Are you responsible for replacing your friend's bicycle? Why or why not?

✱ Once the flat tire has been fixed on your bicycle, would you lend your bike to your friend for transportation?

✱ What problems sometimes arise when friends borrow and lend bicycles, clothing, jewelry, sports equipment, and other things of value?

Choosing a Team

As captain
of a noon league
basketball team,
you have first choice
of players.
Your best friend
is short and
can't pass or shoot
but really wants to be
on your team.

Choosing a Team

* What would you do? What alternatives do you have?

* Is it better to have a basketball team that is made up of friends or one that is made up of skilled players? Is it possible to have both?

* Is there a more objective way to make noon league team assignments? What other ways could you suggest?

* Would letting the kids who are not very good at a sport serve as team captains and choose team members be one good way to resolve this dilemma? Why or why not?

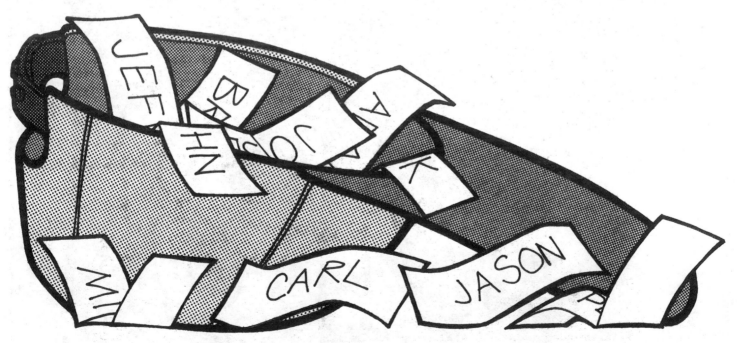

Cheating on a Test

You observe a classmate cheating on a test.

Cheating on a Test

* In what ways does cheating hurt the person who does it? In what ways does it affect other members of the class?

* Would you talk to your friend about what you saw? If so, what would you say?

* Should you let the teacher know what you have seen? Would you feel the same way if the classmate involved was your very best friend?

Living with HIV

A kid in your class
has tested positive for HIV,
the virus that causes AIDS.
He became infected
through a blood transfusion
during surgery some years ago,
before the nation's blood supply
was screened for this virus.
Some of your classmates
are afraid to play
with this kid during recess
or to sit next to him in class.

Living with HIV

* How do you think the boy feels? How do you think your classmates feel when they exclude the boy?

* In what ways might you or your classmates make this boy feel included?

* People are inclined to fear what they do not understand. Do you and your classmates know how the human immunodeficiency virus (HIV) is spread? Would learning more about the virus help? In what way?

Language Barrier

You were raised in another country and don't speak English very well. You have trouble understanding your teacher and keeping up in class.

Language Barrier

* How do you feel about not being able to understand your teacher?

* How would you let your teacher know about your problem, especially if he or she did not understand your language?

* What steps could you take to keep up with the class?

* To whom would you go for help?

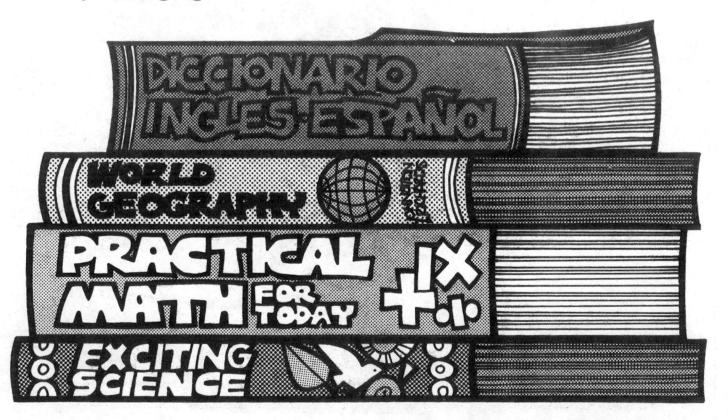

Incorrect Grade

You get an A on a math final. When you check your score, you discover that your teacher added incorrectly. You really should have gotten a B. This will lower your report card grade.

Incorrect Grade

✳ Would you tell your teacher about the incorrect score? Why or why not?

✳ Would your response be different if the error were not in your favor and you got a lower grade than you deserved?

✳ How do you feel about getting a grade you haven't earned?

✳ If you were the teacher, what action would you take if a student came to you with this situation? Would you lower the grade or let the student keep the A?

Out On Your Own

In this section you will find descriptions of situations that may cause conflicts with acquaintances or strangers when you are out on your own. These situations include

following the crowd,

shoplifting,

smoking marijuana,

watching restricted movies,

defending friends,

and damaging property.

First, select and read one of these situations. You can go in any order. Next, think about what you would do. Then, turn the page. Read and consider the statements and questions that are listed. Finally, talk over these ideas with your family. Discuss how you would feel and what you might do in a similar situation.

Forbidden Friend

A classmate whom your parents
have told you to avoid
has asked you to stay after school
and shoot a few hoops.
Both of your parents work
and probably will not find out
if you disobey them.

Forbidden Friend

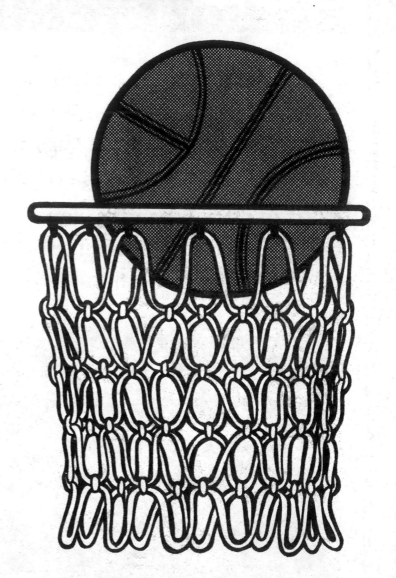

* What might be the consequences of disobeying your parents and doing what they have specifically asked you *not* to do?

* Have you talked with your parents about their reasons for not wanting you to spend time with this classmate? What are their concerns?

* If you do not share your parents' opinion of this classmate, are there some constructive things you can do to change their minds? For example, might you invite this classmate to come over for a visit when your parents are home so that they can get acquainted and, perhaps, see the good qualities you recognize in him or her?

Soccer versus Services

Your soccer team
has qualified for the playoffs.
The first postseason game
is on Saturday.
Your family
regularly attends religious services
on this day.

Soccer versus Services

＊What options do you have?

＊Do you think the game should be postponed?

＊How would you feel about playing in the game instead of going to services? What do you think your family would say?

＊What would you suggest the team or league do to avoid scheduling conflicts of this kind in the future?

PLAYOFF GAME
SAT. JULY 27

Following the Crowd

While you are at a slumber party, someone suggests that the guests sneak out to decorate a neighbor's house with toilet paper. You know that doing so is wrong, but refusing to go along with the crowd makes you feel very uncomfortable.

Following the Crowd

✱ Would you participate? Why or why not? If you didn't participate, what would you tell your friends?

✱ Is it possible that some of the other kids at the party feel as you do? How could you find out?

✱ Have you considered the possible consequences of toilet papering someone's house? Being on someone's property without permission is **trespassing**. What if something gets broken or someone gets hurt? And what if you get caught?

✱ Toilet paper can be very hard to remove, especially if it gets damp and clings to trees and shrubs. Have you thought about what will be required to clean it up? Would you and the other kids who want to "decorate" be willing to help "undecorate" as well?

Unwelcome Touching

Your best friend tells you
that she has a secret.
After making you promise
not to tell,
she confides that her uncle
touches her in ways
that make her feel
very uncomfortable.

Unwelcome Touching

* Sometimes people like to hug and be touched. At other times people are uncomfortable with this level of closeness. Either way is okay. In most instances, the important thing is being able to set limits and to say no. In this instance, the touching your friend is experiencing has gone beyond a simple show of affection.

* What would you do after she confided in you? Would you encourage her to talk to a trusted adult? Whom might you suggest?

* Which is more important, keeping your promise *not* to tell or finding someone to help your friend? If she chose not to talk to anyone, what would you do?

* If you decided to talk to an adult about your friend's problem, to whom would you go? Why?

* What might your friend say or do the next time her uncle approaches her? What would you say or do if someone tried to touch you in the same unwelcome way?

Smoking Marijuana

You are attending a classmate's party.
Someone passes around a joint.

Smoking Marijuana

✳ How does it make you feel to be in this situation?

✳ Would you leave the party? What are some ways of saying no even when friends urge you to say yes to something you don't want to do?

✳ Possessing marijuana is against the law. Why do you think your friends are smoking marijuana? Are people who encourage you to break the law the kind of friends you want to have?

✳ How do you feel about doing something illegal? What if you get caught?

✳ In what ways might smoking marijuana affect your health?

Movie Restrictions

You are spending the night
with a friend
who wants to go to a movie
you know your parents
do not want you to see.

Movie Restrictions

* Would you go to the movie? Why or why not?

* Would you suggest other activities you could do together instead of watching the movie?

* How would you feel about doing something you know your parents would not want you to do?

* What would happen if you watched the movie and your parents found out?

Property Damage

On a steep hill
you jump off your skateboard
to avoid wiping out.
The abandoned board
sails through the windshield
of a neighbor's car.
No one sees the accident
or notices as you retrieve your board.

Property Damage

* Would you tell your neighbor that you are responsible for the broken windshield? If yes, what do you think your neighbor would say?

* Would you offer to pay for the broken windshield?

* In what ways might you earn money to pay for having the windshield replaced?

* If someone damaged your property when you were not around, how would you feel if that person didn't tell you?

On Your Honor

While making change from a twenty-dollar bill,
a clerk gives you a ten instead of a five.
You notice the error immediately,
but *she* does not.

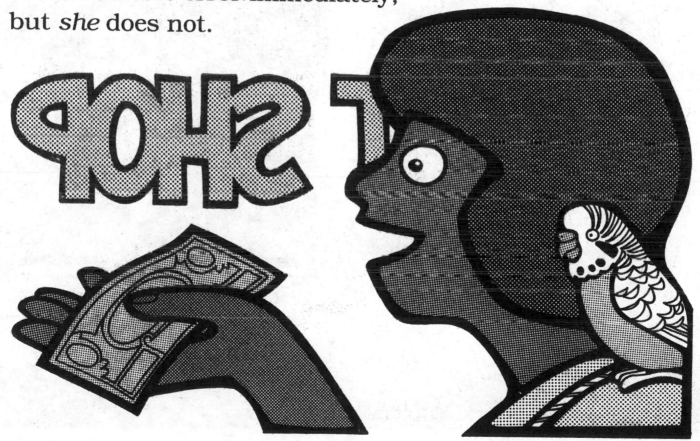

On Your Honor

* Would you call the clerk's attention to the error and return the extra money?

* If you chose not to return the money, would you feel comfortable about keeping it and spending it for something you wanted?

* What might be the consequences to the clerk if her cash drawer comes up short at the end of the day? Might she have to make up the difference out of her own pocket or be penalized in some other way?

* If you were the clerk making change and you made an error, how would you want to be treated? What would you want the customer to do?

Defending a Friend

Your best friend
is extremely overweight.
At a party, you hear some kids
making fun of him.

Defending a Friend

* Why do you think the kids are making fun of your friend? How do you think it makes them feel?

* Would you come to the defense of your friend? If so, what would you say?

* Body shapes differ naturally. Some people carry more weight in proportion to their height than do others. But if your friend is *extremely* overweight, he may have a health problem. Would you feel comfortable talking to him about his weight? If so, what would you say?

Lying About Your Age

If you pretend to be younger than you are,
your dad can get you into a sports event as a child
and will not have to pay
the full adult admission price.

Lying About Your Age

✱ How would this make you feel?

✱ What effect might it have on others if you lie about your age to get admitted for a cheaper rate?

✱ How might your dad react if you asked him to lie for you?

✱ Is the chance to save a few dollars a good reason to be dishonest?

✱ Is it fair for theaters and other venues to charge less for a child than they do for an adult when both occupy the same size seat? Why or why not?

Shoplifting

While shopping with a friend for the holidays,
you see him slip a compact disc into his shopping bag.
You believe that he intends to leave the store
without paying for this CD.

Shoplifting

✳ Is it possible that you have misread your friend's actions and that he has absentmindedly put the CD into the shopping bag and fully intends to pay for it? If so, what might you say to him?

✳ If you are absolutely certain that your friend intends to take the CD without paying for it, is it your responsibility to say something to him about stealing? Why or why not?

✳ Would you tell a store employee? If yes, what would you say?

✳ What might be the consequences for *you* if your friend is caught shoplifting and you are with him?

✳ Would you tell your parents or your friend's parents about this incident? If yes, what would you say?

Being a Vegetarian

You are a vegetarian.
You go to a friend's house for dinner,
where a meal consists of steak
with baked potato, salad, and
garlic bread.

Being a Vegetarian

* Would you eat a few bites of steak or would you just make a meal of the potato, salad, and bread?

* If you choose not to eat the steak, would you explain your reason for not doing so to your host and hostess or simply say no thank you when the meat is passed?

* If you offer no explanation, what would you say if you are asked?

* How could you avoid this situation in the future?

Pocketing the Money

The school band uniforms are in tatters.
To raise money for new ones,
you and a friend are selling tickets
for an opportunity drawing.
Your friend is careless with the ticket stubs,
and you become convinced that she
intends to discard them
and pocket the money that
the two of you have collected.

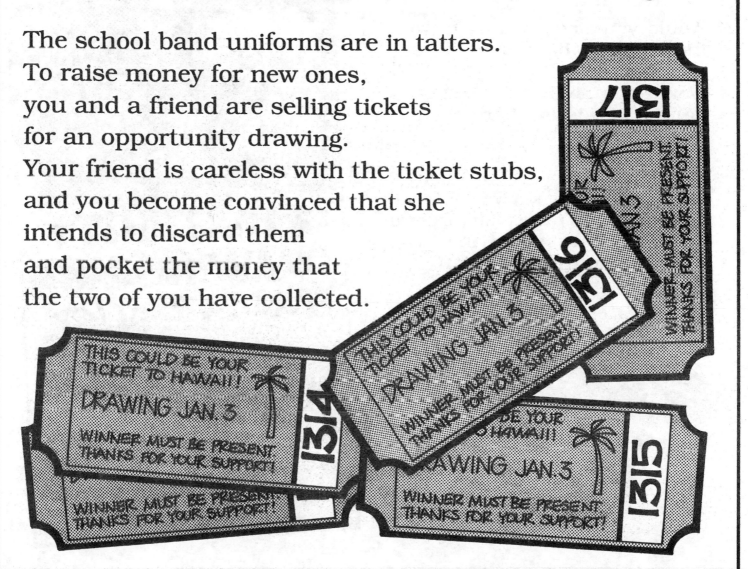

Pocketing the Money

✱ Would you say anything to your friend? If so, what would you say?

✱ Would you notify the teacher or parent who is in charge of this fund-raising activity?

✱ How would the people who bought tickets feel if they knew your friend had kept their money and thrown away their stubs, leaving them with no chance to win a prize?

HIGHLAND HIGH BAND UNIFORM FUND

OPPORTUNITY DRAWING JAN. 3

GRAND PRIZE

A ONE-WEEK TRIP TO

HAWAII!

TICKETS $1.00/ 6 FOR $5.00 AVAILABLE FROM ALL HIGHLAND BAND MEMBERS

Trying New Foods

A classmate invites you to celebrate a holiday with her family. The observance will include a special meal with ethnic foods that are unfamiliar to you. You are curious about your friend's holiday but are hesitant to try foods you have not eaten before.

Trying New Foods

* Would you go to your friend's house? If you went, would you be willing to taste small portions of these foods?

* Have you ever tried a food that looked strange but turned out to be really delicious?

* Would you talk to your friend about your concerns? How do you think your friend would respond? Is there any way your friend could help you feel more comfortable?

Ethnic Jokes

Your family is from another country.
While you are having dinner
at a friend's house,
his father begins telling jokes
which make fun of that country
and its people.

Ethnic Jokes

*Is it wrong to tell jokes that make fun of a country or its people? Why or why not? What harm might jokes of this kind do?

*Why do you think people tell jokes like this?

*When a joke makes you feel uncomfortable, what can you do?

*Would you let your friend's father know how you feel? If your answer is yes, how might you do so? If your answer is no, why not?

*What, if anything, would you say to your friend?

Pirating a Disk

While at a friend's house, you play a fascinating computer game. You would really like to own this game but cannot afford to buy it. Your friend offers to make a copy and give it to you.

Pirating a Disk

✱What are **copyright laws?** What kinds of material do they cover? Whom do the copyright laws protect? Who gets hurt when someone breaks these laws?

✱Does copying a computer disk violate copyright laws? How can you find out what the laws say?

✱Does the number of copies made make a difference? For example, what if only one copy is made?

✱Does the way in which the copies are used make a difference? For example, what if the copies are given away? What if they are sold?

✱Would you be willing to tell your friend that you did *not* want him to copy the disk for you? What would you gain and what might you lose by doing so?

✱Would you accept a copied disk if your friend made one for you despite your strong and clear objections?

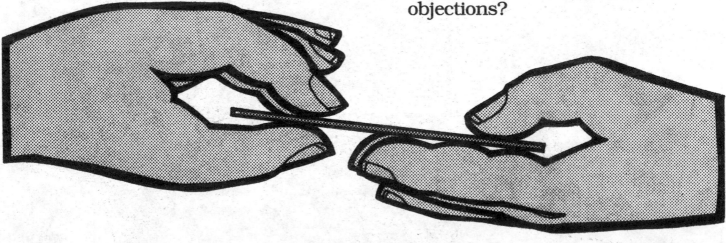

IN YOUR COMMUNITY

In Your Community

In this section you will find descriptions of situations that may cause conflicts among friends or strangers on your block, in your neighborhood, and throughout the wider community. These situations include

breeding animals,

cutting down trees,

dumping toxic wastes,

developing land,

staging a protest,

and trying to improve the neighborhood.

First, select and read one of these situations. You can go in any order. Next, think about what you would do. Then, turn the page. Read and consider the statements and questions that are listed. Finally, talk over these ideas with your family. Discuss how you would feel and what you might do in a similar situation.

Too Many Animals

You want to breed your dog so she will have puppies.
Your parents want to have the dog spayed.
They say that you would not be able
to keep and care for the puppies
and are afraid that you could not find
good homes for all of them.

Too Many Animals

*Why do you want to breed your dog?

*Why do you think your parents want to have her spayed?

*What are some reasons to breed a dog? What are some reasons not to let a dog have puppies?

*If your dog had puppies, what steps would you take to ensure that your puppies have good homes and responsible owners?

*Does the fact that animal shelters are filled with dogs for whom no homes exist influence your feelings or your wishes?

*Does the town in which you live have an ordinance limiting the number of adult animals that can be kept at a single residence? If so, how many dogs are you allowed to have?

*What if there are more puppies than the law allows you to keep? What will happen to the "extra" ones if you cannot find homes for them?

Using Polystyrene Foam

You have decided not to use products
that are made from polystyrene foam
because of the ways in which it
affects the environment.
At a school picnic,
cups made from this substance
are the only ones available.

Using Polystyrene Foam

*Are you concerned about the damage that may be done to the environment by the **chlorofluorocarbons (CFCs)** released into the air during the manufacture of these products? Or are you concerned about the damage done to the environment because these products do not decompose readily and tend to accumulate in landfills?

*Some of the newer plastic foam products are manufactured in ways that are less harmful to the environment, and these newer foams decompose more readily when subjected to the sun's ultraviolet rays. Are you certain that the cups being used at this picnic are the older, more harmful variety? Does it make a difference?

*If you are certain that you do not want to use the cups, what other options do you have?

*Would you say anything to the people who organized the picnic? Would you take any action to encourage them to use other cups at school picnics in the future?

*How could you make the kids in your school and the adults in your community more aware of the problems polystyrene poses for the environment and more willing to explore alternatives?

Helping the Needy

You want to donate twenty-five dollars you have earned to help needy people in your community.

I will work for food. Please help.

Helping the Needy

✱People who are called "needy" really *need* many different things, including food, clothing, shelter, medicine, education, and/or job training. Which of these **needs** would you want to help meet?

✱Would you give cash to someone who appears to need it? Or would you give your money to a charitable group or organization to spend for you? What are the advantages and disadvantages of each of these approaches?

✱If you choose to give your money to a group, would you give all of it to one group or divide it among several?

✱If you give all of your money to one group, how will you decide which one?

✱In what other ways could you help people in need in your community?

Toxic Waste

While playing in a vacant lot near your home, you discover several barrels labeled **toxic**. You realize that the barrels were probably dumped on the lot illegally.

Toxic Waste

✳ What would you do? Whom should you notify so that the barrels will be safely removed from the vacant lot and disposed of properly?

✳ In what ways might the contents of these barrels be harmful to you? To the environment?

✳ What steps can be taken to find out who dumped the barrels on the vacant lot?

✳ Paint, insecticide, and motor oil are toxic substances that are commonly found around the home. In what ways can the "leftovers" from these substances be disposed of so that they do not harm people or the environment? Is it okay to pour them on the ground, flush them down the toilet, or rinse them into the gutter or storm drain? What do you think? Where can you find the answers to these questions?

Cutting Down Trees

You are upset to learn that your city is planning to cut down three beautiful old trees growing on park property because the city cannot afford to rake up the leaves anymore.

Cutting Down Trees

✳ Do you have a right to be involved in the city's decision regarding the trees? Why or why not?

✳ Would you try to get the city to change its decision? How could you do this?

✳ Are there ways the city could handle this problem other than by cutting down the trees?

✳ Sometimes trees must be cut down because they have become diseased or their roots have broken water pipes or damaged pavement. Are you certain that the falling leaves are the *only* reason the city is cutting down the trees? How could you find out for sure?

✳ How could you make other people in your community more aware of the problem?

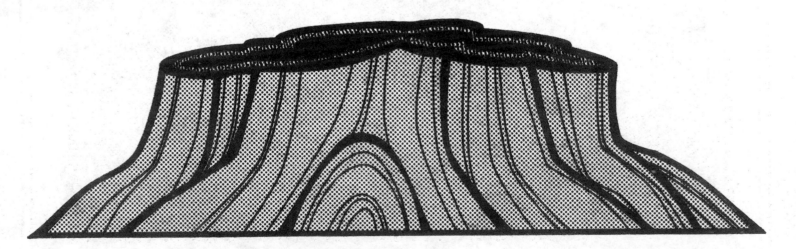

Anti-Semitism

Someone spray-paints
anti-Semitic symbols or slogans
on the front of a store
owned by a Jewish family.

Anti-Semitism

* Why do you think someone would do something like this?

* What would you do about it?

* Whom could you notify—your parents, the shop owners, the police, or some other person or group?

* What should happen to the person who did this?

* What have you done to learn to accept and respect other people and their differences? What more could you do in the future?

Animal Research

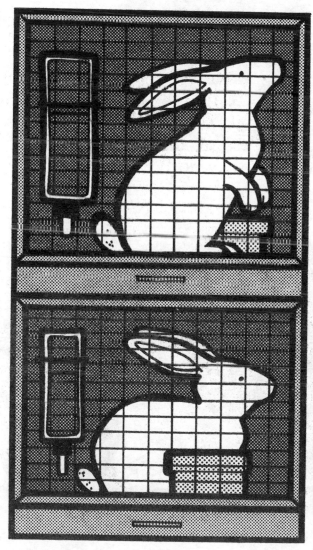

You are concerned about the use of animals in scientific research. When a relative develops cancer, your mother explains that she feels animal research is necessary to find a cure for the disease.

Animal Research

✳ Do you think scientists should use animals in medical research?

✳ If no, does it make a difference in the way you answer if the research would save human lives?

✳ Would it make a difference if the research might benefit a close friend or relative?

✳ Is there a difference between using animals to test cosmetics and using them to test medicines? Why or why not?

Destroying Nature

A developer wants to build
a fifty-unit condominium
on vacant land behind your home.
You spend a lot of time
playing in this wooded area
and have enjoyed observing
the animals that make it
their home.

Destroying Nature

*Who makes decisions about building developments in your community? If you don't know, how could you find out?

*If the developer is entitled by law to build on this land, are there ways you could persuade him or her to lessen the **impact** of this development on your neighborhood? For example, perhaps the condominium project could be designed so that some of the open space remains and some of the mature trees are retained.

*Are there times when it is necessary to destroy animal habitats in order to create human ones?

*How could you get the developer to listen to you? Would you ask neighbors to write letters or sign a petition explaining your concerns?

Staging a Protest

Members of an extremist political group have asked permission to stage a protest through the center of town.

Most of the residents in your community are very much opposed to this group and everything that it stands for.

Staging a Protest

* The U.S. Constitution guarantees to citizens the right to assemble and speak freely. Do constitutional rights and freedoms extend to individuals and groups with whom many would disagree? If you don't know about these constitutional issues, how could you find out?

* In many towns, large gatherings of people require a permit. The reason is that special provisions must be made for traffic and crowd control and for cleanup. Should this group be given a permit? Why or why not?

* If the group is given a permit, what steps can be taken to ensure that the protest is peaceful?

A Better Neighborhood

As one member of a committee,
you must suggest
three things kids can do
to improve the neighborhood.

A Better Neighborhood

* How could you identify the needs of your community? Who could you talk to or what could you read to find out what they are?

* What would your three recommendations be? Why would you pick them? How could they be implemented?

* What can kids do to make a difference in their community?

Six-Pack Rings

While at the beach,
you see a group of adults
carelessly toss several of the plastic rings
that are used to package six-packs.

Six-Pack Rings

✱Under these circumstances, would you say or do anything?

✱In what ways are six-pack rings a threat to birds and other animals?

✱What could you do to ensure that animals are not harmed by these rings?

✱What steps could you take to educate people about the dangers that these rings pose?

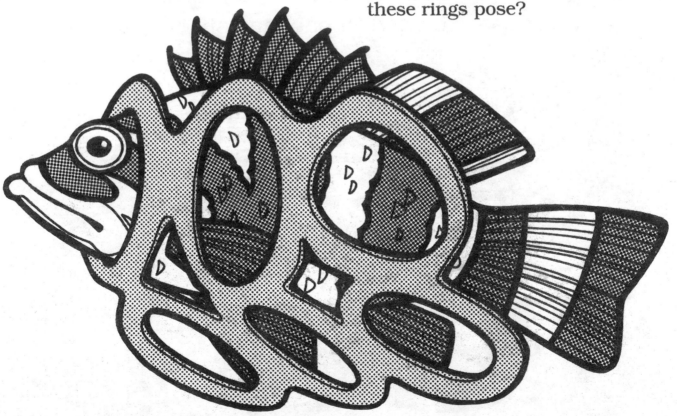

In a Wheelchair

Your new neighbor is in a wheelchair. You are curious about what happened to her and notice that she has difficulty opening doors, going up and down curbs, and shopping in the supermarket.

In a Wheelchair

✳What buildings, sidewalks, and parks in your community might be hard for someone in a wheelchair to enter, use, or enjoy? For example, what about the supermarket or the library? Are the aisles wide enough for a wheelchair? Could someone in a wheelchair reach the top and bottom shelves? And what about your sidewalks? Are there ramps at corners so that wheelchairs do not have to be maneuvered up and down curbs?

✳What improvements have been made in your community to help make public places more accessible to people in wheelchairs? What other steps could be taken?

✳Would you talk to your neighbor about what it is like to use a wheelchair? Do you think your neighbor would like it if you asked questions? What questions would you like to ask?

✳If you saw that someone in a wheelchair was having difficulty reaching something, would you offer to help? Why or why not?

WITHIN YOURSELF

Within Yourself

In this section you will find a collection of tips and lists to help you learn more about yourself and your relationships. These tips and lists cover how to

deal with dilemmas,

resolve conflicts,

make friends,

be a friend,

and express friendship in words and deeds.

HAPPY BIRTHDAY ELIZABETH!

First, read these tips and lists. Next think about the ideas they contain. Then, use these ideas to improve relationships at home, at school, and in your community.

Resolving Conflicts

One thing that makes life difficult and interesting is conflict. **Conflict** is the tension or struggle caused by opposing needs, ideas, wishes, or demands. Conflict can occur between countries or people, between enemies or friends, and even within yourself.

Conflict can cause that uptight, unsettled, and uncomfortable feeling you have when a friend wants you to do something someone has told you clearly *not* to do or when you want to do one thing but know you should do another.

Because conflict is common, you need to know how to deal with it successfully. To **resolve** conflict, you must **make a choice** between the opposing ideas, **seek a compromise** that allows you to combine parts of both ideas or come up with a whole new plan.

Between You and a Friend

When the conflict is between you and a friend, following these steps may help you resolve it.

1. Determine what the disagreement is really about.
2. Decide what you want and what you are willing to give up.
3. Recognize what your friend wants and ask what he or she is willing to give up.
4. Negotiate a compromise that allows each one of you to have *some* of what you want without giving up *all* of what you need.
5. As you negotiate, maintain your own integrity. Set limits and know where you stand. Don't give in or give up on the things that are really important to you. Ask for what you need, be willing to give up something, and then be grateful for what you get.

Within Yourself

When the conflict is within yourself, follow these steps.

1. Identify the choices.
2. Evaluate these choices by considering the advantages and disadvantages of each.
3. Consider the consequences of these choices. With each, what will you gain and what must you give up?
4. Select the one you know is right, the one that offers more advantages and fewer disadvantages, or the one likely to produce fewer unpleasant consequences.
5. Learn from your mistakes. If you resolve a conflict by making a choice you regret, use this experience to help you make a better and wiser choice next time.

Who Are You?

Friendship really starts with you. You need to become acquainted with yourself and feel good about yourself before you can be a friend to others. How well do you know yourself? Read the list of adjectives below. Put a check mark in the box beside each adjective that could be used to describe you *most* of the time. Making these choices will help you understand yourself.

- ☐ academic
- ☐ active
- ☐ athletic
- ☐ bored
- ☐ critical
- ☐ flexible
- ☐ funny
- ☐ happy
- ☐ healthy
- ☐ honest

- ☐ idealistic
- ☐ impatient
- ☐ insensitive
- ☐ kind
- ☐ lazy
- ☐ lonely
- ☐ loyal
- ☐ messy
- ☐ moody
- ☐ neat

- ☐ optimistic
- ☐ outgoing
- ☐ passive
- ☐ patient
- ☐ pessimistic
- ☐ punctual
- ☐ sad
- ☐ scared
- ☐ sensitive
- ☐ serious

- ☐ shy
- ☐ stubborn
- ☐ sympathetic
- ☐ talkative
- ☐ tardy
- ☐ temperamental
- ☐ tense
- ☐ thoughtful
- ☐ tolerant
- ☐ understanding

How Do You Rate As a Friend?

To discover what kind of friend you are to others, mark the answers that best describe you.

	Never	Sometimes	Always
1. I am a good listener.			
2. I talk over misunderstandings.			
3. I try to settle disputes and resolve conflicts.			
4. I apologize when I am wrong.			
5. I congratulate my friends when they do well.			
6. I stand by my friends when they make mistakes.			
7. I help my friends when they have problems.			
8. I stick up for my friends when others tease them or say unkind things about them.			
9. I let my friends know how much they mean to me.			
10. I return the things I borrow in good condition.			
11. I talk about my friends behind their backs.			
12. I embarrass my friends in front of others.			
13. I insist on having my own way.			
14. I brag about the things I own and the things I do.			
15. I criticize my friends in front of others.			
16. I make fun of people who are different from me.			
17. I pick on other kids.			

Tips on Making Friends

While you probably have a few friends already, you may wish to meet some new people and make some new friends. Below and on page 177 are some tips on making friends.

Look inward.
Examine yourself.
What kind of friend
are you?
What kind of person
would you like to have
as a friend?
Do you know someone
who might enjoy
your friendship?

Be yourself.
You want people
to like you
as you are.
Don't put on an act
or pretend to be
something you aren't.
Instead, be natural,
honest, and
sincere.

Be considerate.
Consider the other
person's interests
when you are
making plans.
Consider the other
person's feelings
when you are
talking and
listening.

Tips on Making Friends

While you probably have a few friends already, you may wish to meet some new people and make some new friends. Below and on page 176 are some tips on making some new friends.

Be diplomatic.
Express
your opinions
carefully.
Confront people
respectfully.
Don't criticize
or make
unflattering
comparisons.

Get involved.
Don't let fear
of failure keep you
from trying a new
activity or accepting
a new responsibility.
Shared effort
produces lasting
friendships.

Reach out.
Invite someone
to spend time with you
doing something
both of you would enjoy.
The way to build
friendships is
to share feelings,
ideas, and
experiences.

Hints on How to Be a Friend

Be trustworthy.
When a friend tells you a secret, keep it. Don't repeat it to others. Trust is a vital part of friendship. Loss of trust can destroy a friendship.

Be sensitive.
Be aware of a friend's needs. Try to know when your friend needs to be with you and when your friend wants to be alone. Respect his or her wish for privacy and need for personal space.

Be a good listener.
Kids like to talk to someone who listens actively. Show a genuine interest in the things that are important to your friend.

Be dependable.
If you make a promise to a friend, keep it. Don't let your friend down. Be there for him or her in bad times as well as good. Let friends know they can count on you.

Be honest.
Let a friend know how you feel. If a friend says or does something that hurts you, talk it over with him or her privately. Express your feelings as honestly as you can, and encourage your friend to do the same.

A Friendly Gesture

Do something nice for a friend. Follow one of these suggestions or create a friendly gesture of your own.

Make and send a greeting card to a friend.

Pay your friend a sincere compliment.

Make a treat for your friend's lunch.

Invite your friend to do something fun with you.

Share your favorite book with a friend.

Write a letter to a friend who lives out of town.

Help your friend with a school assignment.

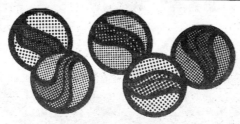

Teach your friend to play a game that you know well.

Call a friend on the phone just to say "Hi!"

Index

A

absence from school, explaining, 81–82
abuse
    drug, 51–52
    sexual, 119–120
access for handicapped persons, 169–170
accident
    bicycle, 83
    skateboard, 125–126
activity, activities
    fund-raising, 138
    keeping track of, 30
    scheduling, 39–40
adults who can help, 52, 108, 120
age, lying about, 131–132
AIDS, 105. *See also* HIV
alcohol, drinking, 53–54. *See also* cigarettes, drugs, marijuana, *and* smoking
allowance, using your, 19–20. *See also* money

animal, animals
    breeding, 147–148
    habitats, 162
    research, 159–160
    six-pack rings and, 167–168
    too many, 147–148
anti-Semitism, 157–158
assignment. *See also* deadline *and* report
    completing an, 33–34
    homework, 37–38
attitudes, racist, 80
audition for school play, 61–62

B

beliefs, 70
betrayal of trust, 72
biases, 65–66, 93–94
bicycle
    accident, 83
    stolen, 99–100
body shape, 130
borrowing, 99–100
breeding dogs, 147–148
bullies, 77–78

C

cancer, 159. *See also* disease
car, fighting in the, 25–26
cash, 152. *See also* allowance, change, *and* money
cash drawer, shortage in the, 128
change, making, 127–128
charitable organizations, 152
cheating on a test, 103–104
chlorofluorocarbons (CFCs), 150
choices, making, 40, 22
choosing a team, 101–102
Christmas pageant, 69–70
cigarettes, smoking, 59–60
clothing, native, 90
competing for a part, 61–62
competition, 61–62
compromise
    on hairstyle, 22
    on loud music, 50
    on TV watching, 30
computer disk, copying a, 143–144
computer game, 143–144

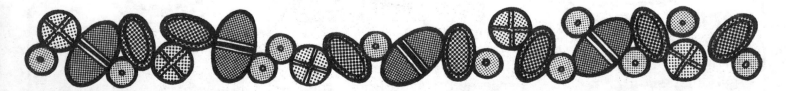

Index
(continued)

conflict. *See also* fighting
  resolution, 173
  schedule, 39–40
consequences, 40
  of a cash drawer shortage, 128
  of shoplifting, 134
  of toilet papering, 118
consideration of others, 50, 176
cooperation, gaining, 50
copyright laws, 144
cosmetics, 160

D

damage
  payments for, 74
  property, 125–126
deadline, missing a, 33–34
dependable, being, 178
development, land, 161–162
diabetes, coping with, 85–86
diet, 86

differences, 93–94
  accepting, 158
  in dress, 89–90
  respecting, 158
diplomatic, being, 177
discrimination, racial, 79–80
disease. *See also* AIDS, cancer, diabetes
  fatal, 23
  research to cure, 159–160
dishonesty, 131–132
disk, pirating a, 143–144
disobedience, 113–124, 123–124
divorce, 31–32
dog, dogs. *See also* puppy
  breeding, 147–148
  sick, 23–24
donations, 152. *See also* gift
dress, native, 89–90
drugs
  parental abuse of, 51–52
  research and, 160

E

environment
  polystyrene foam and the, 149–150
  six-pack rings and, 167–168
  toxic waste and the, 153–154
  trees and the, 156
ethnic
  dress, 89–90
  food, 97–98
  jokes, 141–142
extremist political group, 163–164

F

feelings
  expressing, 24
  hurt, 44
  sparing, 43–44
fighting in the car, 25–26
following the crowd, 117–118
fondling. *See* touching
food, foods
  ethnic, 97–98, 139–140

Index
(continued)

forging a note, 81–82
friend, friends
    defending a, 129–130
    forbidden, 113–114
    how to be a, 178
    rating yourself as a, 175
    things to do for, 179
    ways to make, 176–177
friendship, 36, 87–88, 174
fund-raising activity, 138

G
game
    championship, 57–58
    computer, 143–144
    soccer, 115–116
    softball, 39–40
    video, 35–36
getting involved, 83–84, 177
gift. *See also* donations
    for your mother, 19–20
    unwanted, 43–44
girl friend, dad's, 31
good listener, being a, 178
gossip, 71–72
grade, incorrect, 109–110
    sharing a, 68

grandmother
    things you can do for, 28
    visiting, 27–28

H
hairstyle, choosing a, 21–22
handicapped persons, access
    for, 169–170
help, adults who can, 52,108,
    120
helping the needy, 151–152
HIV, living with, 105–106
holiday
    pageant, 69–70,139
homework, 37–38
honest, being, 178. *See also*
    cheating *and* lying
honor,127–128
human immunodeficiency
    virus (HIV), 105–106
humiliation, handling, 95–96

I
ignored, being, 87–88
improving the neighborhood,
    165–166
involvement, 83–84

J
jokes, ethnic, 141–142

L
language barrier, 107–108
loss of a pet, 24
lying
    about age, 131–132

M
marijuana, smoking, 121–122
mispronouncing a name, 76
money. *See also* change
    deciding how to use, 152
    pocketing, 137–138
    saving, 19
    spending, 19–20
mother, gift for, 19–20
movie restrictions, 123–124
music, loud, 37–38, 49–50

Index
(continued)

N

name, difficult, 75–76
name calling, 63–64. *See also* teasing
nature, destroying, 161–162. *See also* environment
needs
    individual, 152
    neighborhood, 166
needy, helping the, 151–152
neighborhood, improving the, 165–166

O

obesity, 129–130

P

parents, disobeying, 113–114
pet, losing a, 23–24
picking on younger kids, 77–78
plastic, 149–150, 167
political group, extremist, 163–164

polystyrene foam, 149–150
prejudice, 46
prejudiced remarks, 45–46
pretending
    to be sick, 33–34
priorities, setting, 40, 57–58
privacy, respecting, 17–18
promise, promises, 120, 178
property
    damage, 125–126
    respecting, 35–36, 156
    rights, 156, 162
protest, staging a, 163–164
public places, accessibility of, 170
puppy, puppies, 24, 147–148

R

racial discrimination, 79–80
religious
    pageant, 69–70
    services, 115–116

remarks
    insensitive, 95–96
    prejudiced, 45–46
    sarcastic, 65–66
report
    copying a, 91–92
    group, 67–68
resolving conflicts, 173
respect
    for differences, 158
    for privacy, 17–18
    for property, 35–36
right, rights
    to assemble, 164
    property, 156, 162
    to speak freely, 164
role, competing for a, 61–62

S

schedule
    conflict, 39–40
    for watching TV, 42

Index
(continued)

school, schools
    absence from, 81–82
    hurrying to, 83
    vandalizing, 73–74
school play, 61–62
schoolwork. *See*
      assignments,
      deadline, report, *and*
      study habits
secret, secrets, 72, 119
sensitive, being, 178
sharing
    belongings, 18
    a grade, 68
    secrets, 72
    space, 41–42
    the telephone, 47–48
shoplifting, 133–134
six-pack rings, 167–168
slumber party, 117
smoking
    cigarettes, 59–60
    marijuana, 121–122

soccer game, 115–116
softball game, 39–40
space, sharing, 41–42
study habits, 37–38

T
tardy, being, 84
teacher,
    biased, 65–66
    insensitive, 95–96
team, choosing a, 101–102
teasing, 63–64, 97–98
television
    place for watching, 41–42
    rule against, 29–30
test, cheating on a, 103–104
testing
    cosmetics, 160
    medicines, 160
thoughtlessness, 50
toilet papering a house,
    117–118
touching, unwelcome, 119–120
toxic waste, 153–154
travel by car, 25–26
trees
    cutting down, 155–156
    preserving mature, 162

trespassing, 118
trip, car, 25–26
trust, 72
trustworthy, being, 178

U
understanding yourself, 174

V
vandalism, 73–74, 157
vegetarian, being a, 135–136
video game, playing a, 35–36
views, biased, 93–94
visiting grandmother, 27–28

W
waste, toxic, 153–154
wheelchair, using a, 169–170

Y
yourself
    being, 176
    getting acquainted with,
      174
    understanding, 174

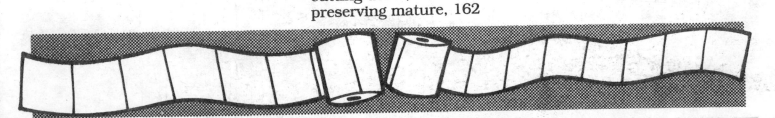